The Origins of Streams

poems by

Rachel Economy

Finishing Line Press
Georgetown, Kentucky

The Origins of Streams

*For the ones who speak with the soil,
and who listen when it sings*

Copyright © 2021 by Rachel Economy
ISBN 978-1-64662-403-4 First Edition
All rights reserved under International and Pan-American Copyright Conventions. No part of this book may be reproduced in any manner whatsoever without written permission from the publisher, except in the case of brief quotations embodied in critical articles and reviews.

ACKNOWLEDGMENTS

"where the wound is" originally published in *Dark Mountain,* Issue XI, Spring 2017

"Where Things Come From" originally published in *The Round,* Issue IV, Spring 2011

"Grand Canyon" and "Relationship" originally published in *Faults,* an Index/Fist 'zine, August 2013

"Summer" and "Air" originally published in *7 Poems I wrote for _____.* February 2018

"A Home for the Seeds" originally published in *Dark Matter Women Witnessing*, Issue V, June 2017

"Herd" and "root supper" originally published in *Watershed*

Publisher: Leah Huete de Maines
Editor: Christen Kincaid
Cover Art: Rachel Economy
Author Photo: Riv Ranney Shapiro, Sacred Witness Media
Cover Design: Elizabeth Maines McCleavy

Order online: www.finishinglinepress.com
        also available on amazon.com

Author inquiries and mail orders:
Finishing Line Press
PO Box 1626
Georgetown, Kentucky 40324
USA

Table of Contents

Storyteller Thumbs 1

Summer 2

where the wound is 3

storm 4

Crevices I & II 5

Signals 6

The Buoyant Potato Manifesto 8

Dragonfly Tactics 10

Red 12

coasts 13

Air 14

Relationship 16

Grand Canyon 17

Tangled Songs and Other Talk 18

American Chestnut 19

If There Is No Dancing 20

Dry 22

the wings of man 23

Culinary Escapism 24

Carve 26

Where Things Come From 27

The Astronomical Vaginal Fluids Manifesto 28

an epic mythology 29

Faulty Chain 30

root supper 31

Herd 32

A Home for the Seeds 33

Storyteller Thumbs

It was all just a giant scheme for dancing. There was no primordial soup. No big bang. What there was, was a dancehall. What there was, was a clearing in the woods with the distance between bodies fluctuating wild and the birds cranky and clattering in the trees. What there was, was the sound of cellulose and drums. What there was, was the ocean inside of every thing, was every particle inside a salty wave.

It was like this: somehow, in the beginning, which was not a beginning because the concept of time hadn't been born (or had it), well, in the beginning and from then on and still and always, the atoms were in love with each other's skin, which was actually not skin but an electric field. And the atoms were in love with their own centers, which were not actually centers but selves that couldn't stay in exactly one place.

What happened, or happens, or is happening, or will happen, is: matter wanted to dance. To separate and re-embrace. To differentiate, to sing solitary songs, and to amalgamate and merge. To scream alone in the midnight hallway, to make love in the sun of the river until skin dissolves. It was critically huge and slightly yellow. It was terribly mundane. Matter is always doing this: food, breath, cells, shit, soil, stones, coal. Eating, dying, fucking, sitting next to other bodies breathing on the train, eating dirt, exchanging cells and selves and pieces and peaces. Pull apart and come together. A dance move as young as time.

And then one day, which could be tomorrow for all we know, matter woke up in the ecstasy of this dance. And it was full of longing and the sizzling light. And it wanted to witness itself. It wanted to watch the dance while dancing, to sing about it while stepping and kicking and rattling the universe's floor. And so matter grew a mouth full of senses, a monkey with a storyteller in its thumbs. The soil wanted to know itself and so it birthed a thousand tongues and teeth.

And those tongues and teeth and thumbs, they thought they were there just to tell how things were, or are, or will be. Simply to describe.

But they were mouths still and always kissing shale and stalactites and the spines of sea urchins. They were matter and its witness, both. And every time they opened to tell the tale of the dancehall, of the drumming, of the clearing in the trees, they changed its shape. And in so doing, they also changed their own.

Summer

I want summer the way that it can be
hot and full of peaches, bright
sun-yellowed kitchens and walks
to nowhere but sitting down on the curb half
way to drink a coffee we shouldn't
have gotten but it was clicking with fresh ice, then
dancing madly when the jitters hit in the middle
of the fruit-heavy street. I want
lovers and cinnamon cake, I want
to move towards you when you dance and twine
around the air that you twine around, I want
knot-tying competitions from summer camp
but on the steps of my porch with the smell of
salt in our fingers from the ocean, I want
the ocean, I want
to be hurled belovedly from sea to sand by
wave after wave, my body inside, I want
to arrive on the beach laughing and
only slightly scraped, to find
you on a blanket laughing as
you cut open a mango, stand
and move towards me, with
sweet juice dripping from
your perfect, outstretched hand.

where the wound is

where the wound is you can see map lines if you look close. where the wound is rivers leak out. where the wound is, I place bundles of chewed plantain, stem the outpour, check dams made to keep the streams from gobbling out their own flesh banks. where the wound is I scrub salt so forgetting won't come.

often I confuse my body with a mountain range. often I confuse you with a fishing pole, pellet gun, the tines of a fork. it is always more dangerous to paint the gaps, gaping, to call out with the mouth of a cut thigh or elbow, to say I need I need I bleed look hear the anger and the hemoglobin howl.

where the wound is, it is clear: the world ails so body ails too. our skin is only as impermeable as anything else: soil, leaves, sky. all things move into each other, this is called the atom, this is called your pulmonary system, this is called shit, this is called tomatoes, this is called the San Andreas, this is called cells, this is called morgues and mountains I—

—confuse my body with a mountain range. where the wound is, if you look real gentle, you can see map lines to the next world. they are fragmented, broken and quiet, dangerous thing: to say I need, I need, I bleed.

storm

cyclone in your gut, girl, swing
heavy towards the wall with your scapula, un-
balanced, blanched cheeks blending
aura too fine a term for sudden
blindness and the stabbing numbness
of a left hand, your
heart, your
heart, your
heart
is not under attack, girl, it's
your head in the river, girl, it's
your head in the riptide, girl, it's
your head in the storm.

stop.
slow, re-
turn to the bread bowl.
stir.
turn.
rise.
repeat.
sing songs, poorly
today, sing songs
of rising
from wreckage and burn
from migraines the size of
shift, of
continental plates.

fold.
knead.
repeat.
sometimes
the only prayer you can manage
is baking bread
for the first time in three years
under the rain that's come finally
and behind it, somewhere
the hidden light of the finally full moon.

Crevices I & II

I. Orifice

You are a mouth. Gulp, ginger snare fire, red, blood flank, layers of inner cheek sanctum, stalagmite richness and steam. Tonsils flounder, river gone down, deep deep deep oh. You are a mouth, holy scent and hunger. Huddling, hunkering down. Holds me, whether I want or no, reaches out and grabs with that insidious, sweet heavy-sweat tongue. Did you floss today? Did you examine the crud in between the pearls? All the shit and stagnance we've collected here? You are a mouth. You talk a good game. You reel, you swagger and sweet talk and mean talk me in, you are a uvula circus. You pass mirrors before my eyeteeth. Our canines clash, how could you? Hammer, hammer throat, you are always hitting me over the head with horrible cages or unexpected bread. You are too sharp and too sweet and I can trust neither. On early mornings which are really late nights, I try to walk under the dark of the new moon and curse your name. You are the cave, you are the teeth, you are the sugar bumps and the salt on my burning tongue.

II. Cave

There's something else running. Other side of the peaches. I can almost see, far from here, just on the other side of the peaches. See it? About the shape of a bobcat. Like that one time on the deck, the hidden deck in the woods, where we lay impatient, waiting for the stars to go up so we could see just enough to spelunk down into each other's voiceboxes. Throat cave jumping, looking for the origins of streams. That one time on the hidden platform and fir when you pulled up your shirt and showed me the door in your breastbone. I was distracted for a moment by the sight of your nipples but then I saw there was a sudden archway, an opening there between. And I leaned forward slow slow. And I looked through the doorway in your chest. And what looked out at me, like it might spring. Oh. Oh what looked out, was huge and feline and wild, arrogant and ruff-maned and gold. Oh what a mountain of a thing, not lion but full of bladed lips, oh g_d what terrible beauty you keep in there, beating like it's just for the sake of your blood, like it couldn't, if it wanted, just up and devour me whole.

Signals

Today my kitchen filled with bees and the sky was made of smoke.
I sneezed seven times walking home. Earlier
I let the two bees that were not trapped, unreachable
in the stove fan hood vent, out
one at a time. I waited
until they landed on the window, then
coaxed each into a mason jar, covered
the mouth with brown paper, scurried
to the porch steps and turned the mouth up, open
to the not-yet-smoky sky. One
of the bees came easily, flew
free, the second
got caught when I tried to save her
between the glass of the jar and the glass
of the window pane, her leg
may or may not
work again.

How do I know
if I have done more harm or good? Why
would a hive break itself
to come and buzz against my ear, bones
the sky
is full of smoke, a return
to the season of California when I search
the internet using the phrase "What
is on fire this time?"

I used, as a child
to be freeze-stun frightened
of bees.

I changed.
I became someone who could fill a metal cone
with smoke, contained this time, someone
who could borrow honey, who could
check for breaches in the hive. I let
bees land on me, I freed them from
spider webs. I don't
know how, but
I changed.

It is the same type of terror now, though, when
I look at you and imagine saying something. My body
a sky on fire, my body
a small child trapped
in a tiled room
full of furious alarm, buzzing, buzzing–
I can't remember if I want
to kiss you
or run
everything smells like clover
and hillsides full of flames.

The Buoyant Potato Manifesto

Oh what we wouldn't give
for a buoyant spud
for that thick sweet packet of starch
with its hours and hours
bled into our hands
stems mounded and
mounded and
mounded
weekly
lovingly
with soil until
those stems become roots
that bulge and brim with
all-knowing eyes.

Oh what we wouldn't give
for that buried russet nugget
to float effortlessly
with unbent backs
unburnt necks
and tubers unsliced
by shovel's silver bite and gleam

to come clean
to come up
soil crumbling
away
to come cooked, and
tender, to come
roasted
perfectly done.

What wouldn't we give?

Nothing, except
that this digging
it makes our backs sore but
it makes them strong, this
bending
it gets soil in our nail beds and
in between our teeth until

we remember with the chewing of grit that
nobody and
nothing
escapes without
the harvest-ton heavy
wretched grace
of becoming
someone else's food.

And thank g_d anyway
for the shovel's slice
so there are potatoes
unfit for the terrible perfection
of this thing we call market
food that never touches money, simply
dirt, shovel, hands, box
water, fire
tongue.

Someday
they will try to sell us
a patented run
of anti-gravity seed spud slices.

Then we will turn our
shovels from the ground.
Then we will dig
everywhere that is necessary
to keep them from replacing
this rough and only divinity
with food that is already chewed.

Dragonfly Tactics

there is an article traveling around
that I admit I haven't read, called
something like: female
dragonflies play
dead
to avoid the unwelcome advances
of male dragonflies. Friends
are posting this with
smiles, comments
about feminism and
great tactics learned from nature and, besides
my intense misgivings
about the history of
how science has used the word
"natural" to talk
about gender and the ways we
make choices about
who and when we fuck, I

know so many
women
and
humans, with
so many muscled wings beating
beauty across the windy sky
who have had to use
dragonfly tactics
like this
to get out
and it was
fierce and
necessary and
powerful and it
belonged to us that we did that and I

 will celebrate those humans
to the ends of the earth, but I
don't
want to celebrate
a world
built on the circumstances

that necessitate the stilling
of gossamer wings
in which that is the conversation's end
in which we have
to pretend we are nothing
dead, gone
annihilated
in order
to be free

Red

I.   red
freckled evening and the sea
gray flecked gulls
in your eyes wend
between the foreground
and storm's fast approach
I don't remember
how to write a poem
but I know your hair
was red.

II.   some slight potatoes
might explain (you)
but clocked into your visions
remain music and music's parts
I sit in red blankets
compare my bravery to yours
crystallize that and
salt your dinner.

III.   the light plays inconstancies
cross page and 'tween
the sheets of skin you call your other arm.
there is nothing of you, I speak
to a mirror and crave apples
something sweet to blame.

IV.   four little muskrats
(of which we knew nothing)
slipped past backyard periphery
invisibility only matters to the skeptics
and who, then
to call ourselves children
of the trees?

this will be no easy redemption
bodies wont to bleed throng
the forest
such a trial, to keep our holy hands
free and down
among the saplings
not nailed to the curtains of the pines.

coasts

no matter
how many times
I try to stitch one ocean
to the other
they remain a mouth
full of mountains, a continental
division
apart. every
time someone falls off the glass edge
of existence, I
am always on the wrong side
of the watershed
calling long-distance
thundering tears that fall
on the other side of the ridge
from yours.

Air

Tonight I gave myself
the Heimlich while naked, thrown
over the back of a chair (having
aspirated somehow
a tincture, magic I tried
to slip under my tongue
to make up for the long nights of
searching for self instead of sleep). I
had just stepped out
of the shower.

Suddenly
where time for decisions
about asking for help and
the utter vulnerability of skin
was once endless, or
nearly so, I
now found
only thirty seconds
between myself and
the finite convulsion of lungs.

If the chair had not worked
(and as it was I had to go back twice, twice
I could not breathe the slightest)
if the chair had not worked
I would have run onto the porch naked
and hammered on the neighbors' door in the moth-bitten light
of cool June, and someone
maybe
would have wrapped their arms around me
so I could have air again.

Maybe not.

The absurdity of this situation strikes me like
the absurdity of all need, how
I have wanted
for months
to slide closer to the idea
of your arms wrapped around me, how

I have therefore run
in the opposite direction, thinking
time is endless, thinking
there will be another day, later, when
it's safer, to
clamor onto the stark exposure of
porch steps at night, to
splay myself, epidermis and heart showing,
begging
give me air
give me air
give me air.

Relationship

I think you're wrong about almost
everything
except
the way you press me into the door.

Grand Canyon

These are the colors of the hole where the sea used to live:

Rust. Ochre. Mottled blue. Beige strips through speckled brown, the hue of a horse path several fathoms down. She walks the canyon. Thinks about organs and sediment, the shapes around cavities, the arc of an emptiness. It does not feel lonely. A solid lack. That salt ground, it took eons to get this way. In a ledge overhead, hidden behind scrub trees that grow one inch every 500 years, images shift like dried blood on sandy rock. Everywhere in the walls the wind writes its name, over and over, susurrating, narcissus, unable to tear itself away from the empty caverns that let it hear itself, calling back its own name.

I have this canyon-heart, baby, all organ and sediment. Empty the way a bell peals in a cave. Utter room. I build these arms out of what's left of oceans from before the continents grew up and got jobs. It took me eons to get this way and I need the space. It does not feel lonely. You think it should. That I should ache for you, that the waves only receded yesterday, that the taste of saltwater is still strong on my tongue. You stand too close to my edge with your camera and thirst, trying to see water, trying to capture my far-off other side. Step back. I drove past rivers and cotton fields to get to this imaginary water. At the gas station in Mississippi they did not like my haircut, but that is another knife for another day.

It wasn't that I left you. It's just that your organs, they are full of blood and noise, a river valley, the lush hills in autumn. Pours into me and I don't want. To be an ocean again. You say you would like to fiddle spin and so you need me. Darling I have already flown, I shut the windows in the desert and didn't answer any phone calls or echoes save my own. I became layers that mapped backwards with the sun, to a time full of gills, to the sound of froth, frontrunner waves gone, memory silhouettes that I keep in this crevice of a chest and when you get so close we both end up choking on saltwater ghosts.

Tangled Songs and Other Talk

Start early and tell no one
The earth falls towards a sun
Ruby, like her hair
Gravel road sings smoke to the tires
You watch her eyes trying
To reign in the rambling sky
And dismantle everything.
You, strangers who know both bodies
Like a child knows the sunrise
Shock of color, red never existed before now
But tomorrow red will come again
Come singing and
Maybe safety is a song revolving
And free is tar-tough, like the road
Maybe it too flames and bursts,
Maybe, like the sun between the slender pines.

American Chestnut

so you
bring this blight here and then complain
of cholera in your heartwood, heavy
solitude within solitude's vast refrain
the absence of branches to hold your sound.
and by the hypnotic light
of sun spread across the sky
entranced, you find a self
personable and alone among the soil.
bend at the waste, knees
dust cast from your joints
spread your fingers into
verdant wood and majesty, gone
from eastern hills, and remember
an epidemic, what it meant
for your side of the sky.

If There Is No Dancing

If there is no dancing
the revolution will not come.
If there is no dancing
the sunflowers will curl in
on their heavy heads too early,
stars bound straight for red death
no chance to feed the curious mouths
of children or birds.

If there is no dancing
Your ears will not hear my
tongue-song drumming
I will not know
what sound your body makes.

If there is no dancing
the revolution will stay too long
calling itself progress and
turning pale
a death un-coming
un-feeding
un-found.

If there is no dancing
our hammer-hearts
cannot feel the nail.

Once,
the hive-minded painters
walked out of the fields
and into the local bar
to ask why everyone was singing.
The people looked over their glasses
over swaying heads
and said:
song is the only choice
when the soil voice gets hit
with helicopter fire.
What do you do when everything
is coming up orange?
How else will you un-lid your eyes
and not turn and run?

Alone,
I open up landscapes of the possible
behind my eyes, like
we could walk speakers into
the parking deck and mad
dance stamp until
the rains redistribute the waters
or until
we are declared a wild nuisance
or until
the mud-slung
hateful shape of things
grows us another hammer and
another hand to hold it and
we write songs that say
what will be built out of
houses, coastlines
reef-depths that now stand broken.

We could kiss like the abandoned
so that nobody would be.

We could write songs on the bark of a tree
without touching it.

We could overlap and balance,
invisible wings touching
twisting to vestigial beats.

We could reopen the sunflowers
petal by bright sky petal
until they too dip their heads
into music and move
until they too can turn faces
towards the horrors and hurts.

If there is no dancing
we will never remember
how to turn the rusting wheel.

Dry

In August we ran out of gas
black trash bag billows obscured
first: premium, then super
finally the pavement stood
dirty and abandoned
a disappointing dog thrown to the roadside
because the grass wouldn't grow
under its runoff, stark yellow.

Lonely gas stations imposed themselves
on our peripheral vision, side mirrors
garish, hunched harbingers
of the empty tank apocalypse
with each drive we felt it coming:
immobility's doom.

And it was only the hulking city
beautiful, fragmented
evaporated and afraid
of her own waters,
who felt the desperate ache for oil
and was soon salvaged
and sent on her way, high way
to octane bliss.

But in the house on Westminster
we recalled the '96 Olympic
influx, when
millions descended
on the sticky southern summer
and emissions went down.
We panicked for traffic,
for fuel and travelers, fanatic, then
we found we all remembered
how to ride the trains.

the wings of man

nefarious possession
a watercolor done in red, our
afternoon waned among flying machines.
realization's return: you, grounded to center,
still lay claim to several organs,
internal,
I thought were all my own.
counted, each turning screw—
gear—change and twisted to
aim's ultimate child, discovery.
please reiterate: what it is we
came here to claim; or
how grass leaves and pages, ancient
poets quiet—write for me to love you with
any grace I find, or even
why it is your hand touches
only the air apart from mine.

Culinary Escapism

Drawn in pen and ink,
double dimensions, the streets
are full of you (workmen dig
bulldozer-holes, redirect
traffic and innocence, policemen
come in to borrow
our microwave, are informed:
> the appliances cannot function in
> simultaneous rhythm, blow
> a circuit, flip back to "on"
> start again).

Sautee: kale, carrots, garlic. Slow
simmer beneath breastbone, gut
how long for a reaction to move
to completion to move to
a new city and do everything alone.

Grab iron, a skillet cast
hot and heavy to burning
palm. Save your food and
where do things come from these days?

Carrots growing in the supermarket.
(Drop me, burnt skillet fingers
unjust and scattered in
ancient linoleum dust).

Underneath this: the face of
his dying, reborn in thought
second, am devastation, am
lunch fallen to feet, what to believe

when death comes sudden? Burnt
slight holes between ribs, fingers.

Boys at 31 can't seem to stay alive.
The grave robbers come to steal flowers, bulldogs—
are you angry at my idiotic wanders
so far to the north?
Punish the messenger

without news nothing has happened yet.

The ground is sated and content
here without you
the wind has picked back up
and the fridge overflows with cabbage
and friends turn, strange and over, and
the winter is still cold.

Carve

You handed me a cedar fragment
I locked it in my chest
And held the scent of closets
Nests of wood and wool spun
Out into my years
(Which I seem to keep acquiring)
Things that smell of safety
Dust and home
The trust to hold you
But a dowel turns in cedar
Speaks of coal
Friction into fire, stolen
From the forests or the gods
And I am stolen, you—
Twist the trees
Unknowing and I
Am wood smoke in your palms.

Where Things Come From

On Sundays I go to church in the kitchen
summer hatpins and
apple crisp with the bruise-baby fruits
accidental afternoons eaten
up with chatter, oats
buttered pan-slip to hands
in the dough.

And the loaves abound in
sideboard baskets
linoleum re-creation of rising love
like home's mimicry, soft and
honest, almost
like G_d is talking to the farmers
gone turnip-happy and over, gotta
speak when the spirit moves and
gotta eat when she says supper's on.

The Astronomical Vaginal Fluids Manifesto

It was incredible
how much liquid
came out.

An ocean with legs in it
a slick grey pitcher's mouth
made from side stream clay mud
pouring the scent of estuary in.

It wasn't a one-time thing
no instantaneous delight
no sudden mattress river
no event to precede.

It was simply
a cauldron bent
on beating back
the drought
all those chests and tomato throats
shriveling
from how much
we do not talk
about the ecstasy
of this kind
of water.

an epic mythology

turtle done in grey
inquisition
the world in a range
of cupboard and shell
whale bones on a wooden board.

this is the place
where we keep the animal bones
formaldehyde
taxonomic cabinetmakers
the lovebirds nuzzle in a feathered corner
this is how we order the
dusty eons' magic.

she asks: if death comes easy
once all is scale and bone
and *coral*, I say, *a difference*
of entirety
the inanimate curls of skeleton in the
shape of brain, vital, waste
is not a word in soil
language, learned.

she asks: what is to be done
in the face of all things
reverb of supermarket purchase
and our footprints in the streams, and
the thrill of gardens
corner pigeons' conversation
taxidermy's smile
as if the city were no different
as if here too we can still
make out the sky.

Faulty chain

1. I watch your fingers twist in the WD-40, wring and ready bike parts, change delicate bearings, rolling nubs of bike body. I wish I were tied to the bike stand. I wish it was me you were working on.

2. Go to hell. Your banjo sounds like the screws in my head coming loose, cranial mass leaking through the cracks, scrambling, did I love you, were we foxes in the north meadow, was I tangled wired wearing thin and cranked in the hinge of your door?

3. I imagine you as a rough red patch of road. I get out of my bucking car and lay fresh gravel over the pothole of you. Then I drive on through, out, away, manzanita only and sky.

root supper

I concede to your salient design
strewn and stratified
aligned into oven mitt and glass.
I confuse the matter:
turnip troubled
salty and vivacious between
the sticky coalescence
of oil, grains, plate
remain careful of convection
attain the highest taste.

Herd

Remember the day we awoke from a warm nap
hiking across scattered boulders and yellow wildflowers we couldn't
legally pick,
to startle the far away elk cresting the ridge.
Remember
how their bodies, grey-brown, the bark of pine trees back home
moved in some shifting flux over the hill, coming ever toward,
ever toward.
Remember the sharp breath we held in the thin air
that our lungs weren't used to yet,
bringing the vague memory that we once lived in
some other, lower,
stationary place.

Remember,
how across the air they were as close to us as our own
blood, dancing in our veins,
how they poured over the hill
two hundred in our one-held-breath's time?
Remember the way they turned to us, and stared
as we emerged over our own hilltop, smelling of ten days
and that last, icy lake,
and how they continued toward, ever-staring
and how wild we felt
and how they seemed so unafraid.

A Home for the Seeds

It was as the floods were coming in and the steam burning through the windows that we gripped our spades in our teeth and climbed into the mouth of the mountain to build secret homes for the seeds.

We did not know each other, or we thought we did not.

We had not been born in the same places. We had never spoken words the others recognized. In the flood, trying to get out of the city, we had found ourselves in a tangle of unmatched tongues and car tires spinning wretched against the finally wet, so wet, too wet soil. Cacophony. An unwieldy din.

But there was a language we held common, a thing that drove us madly into the hills soaking and coughing, our pockets full of sunflowers and fava beans. Call it the language of fertility. The rhetoric of rot. Of reimagining. Call it insanity. Call it a failure to bite down and trudge the proper path and save the proper thing. Call it disease or dis-ease or dissonance or dismantling, all.

Whatever name, we had it. We were, first and foremost, the ones who got out, some privilege and a dash of chance. And we were also ones who knew that the story of what-to-do-in-case-of-disaster was a made thing, a stitched thing, an invisible law book, something written by five-fingered-hands in one very specific language for one very specific purpose. That the disaster itself was a story too, a real thing, yes, and a real thing that had been made, a written thing. And we were the ones who knew story could, just as truly, be torn up, dug up, re-stitched, by hands, by briars, by sharks' teeth snagging. We were the imaginers. The anxious creators, for whom no law was obvious and no story a static end. We had no set idea of how precisely to respond to a flood. We were not wed to any particular conversation with G_d about the monogamous needs of animals on large boats that wait out storms. Neither were we looking to save the microwaves.

And we were the ones who had no children. Or whose children had already gone. To the waters, to the white and hungry guns, to the longing. We were the ones who had no seeds.

So we found some. In the backs of our closets, in the corner stores standing ankle-deep in water, in the jars on the tilting kitchen shelves. And we gripped our spades in our teeth, and we looked sideways as the streets began to buckle and fold into foothills, and we saw each other limping, and rolling, and running, pockets spilling over with hard-shelled children, with descendants of future trees, and we reached out as we ran, and we gripped each other's hands in our hands.

It was the queerest thing, like a bird in love with a sturgeon, a family of defectors, arms empty of objects and pockets emptied into soil above the water line, saving no wealth or infrastructure, saving the wrong things. A re-kindling, a re-kinning, a reckoning.

All this dying, it has been beyond swallowing.

All those bodies, they came home to the soil. And so we gave them children. Hard-shelled and root-bound. It was a kind of making love to the dead. We slipped seeds into their pockets. Their bodies fertile, already almost soil, meeting the beans, the walnuts, the pits we plunged into the wet ground. The rhetoric of rot. The true nature of kinship: all things becoming other things. Hidden in the mountain, learning each other's languages, guarding, gardening, waiting for the first roots, those parts of the plants called "radical," to unfurl their faces into the soil.

Rachel Economy is a poet-performer, ecological educator, design-thinking strategist, and gardener. She is the owner of Index For The Next World, an online hub of story-publication, skills-education, and human-centered design consulting for those seeking to build a world that thrives. Rachel holds a master's degree in Social Innovation and Sustainability from Goddard College, with a concentration in Transformative Language Arts and a master's thesis exploring narrative re-design as a part of social change and ecological justice. She teaches gardening, needs-based design, systems thinking, writing & performance, permaculture, group facilitation, maker & homesteader crafts, and embodied nature connection skills to all ages, in rural and urban settings. Her poetry and other writing can be found in *Dark Mountain, Animal: A Beast of a Literary Magazine, Dark Matter Women Witnessing,* and various other publications. You can find more of Rachel's writing and work at www.indexforthenextworld.com.

www.ingramcontent.com/pod-product-compliance
Lightning Source LLC
LaVergne TN
LVHW041604070426
835507LV00011B/1307